NATURECRAFT

LOOK WHAT
I DID WITH A LEAF!

MORTEZA E. SOHI

WALKER AND COMPANY
NEW YORK

First published in the United States of America in 1993 by Walker Publishing Company, Inc.; this paperback edition published in 1995

Published simultaneously in Canada by Thomas Allen & Son Canada, Limited, Markham, Ontario

The Library of Congress cataloged the hardcover editions of the book as follows:
Sohi, Morteza E.
Look what I did with a leaf! / Morteza E. Sohi.
p.   cm. — (The NatureCraft series)
Summary: Provides examples of different kinds of animals that can be made out of leaves and suggests various uses for the finished product.
ISBN 0-8027-8215-9 (cloth). — ISBN 0-8027-8216-7 (reinforced)
1. Nature craft — Juvenile literature.   2. Leaves — Juvenile literature.   [1. Leaves.   2. Nature craft.   3. Handicraft.]
I. Title.   II. Series.
TT160.S57   1993
745.58′4 — dc20   92-35142
CIP
AC
ISBN 0-8027-7440-7 (paper)

Book design by Leslie Bauman

Printed in Hong Kong

12 13 14 15 16 17 18 19 20

Have you ever really looked at leaves? In the fall they shout **Look at me** with crunchy, crackling noises in bright reds, oranges, and yellows. And then one day in the spring you suddenly notice everything is lush and green because the leaves have pushed out all over the trees.

It's wonderful to see so many leaves at once, but such bounty keeps us from taking the time to stop and look at just one. Making animals with leaves is an adventure that will open your eyes to each leaf's special beauty!

The first step in making leaf animals requires a few steps on your own—outside. Take a bag or a shoe box and go on a leaf hunt. Leaves are all around you—in backyards, parks, and along city streets. Once you start looking for them you won't be able to stop finding them. Look for leaves that are different sizes, different shapes, and different colors.

Dos and Don'ts

- Do remember to look for very tiny leaves. You'll need them for eyes, noses, beaks, and feet.
- Do take time after your walk to rinse and press the leaves. If you wait too long, your leaves will become brittle and curled.
- Don't get greedy. Someone else may be on a leaf hunt too. Don't take more than you can clean and press that day.
- Don't hurt the trees and bushes. Taking a leaf won't hurt anything, but avoid breaking twigs and branches.
- Don't take leaves off trees that are on private property without getting permission.
- Do have fun!

Spring and Summer

In the spring and summer most of the leaves you will find are green, but as you'll see, there are lots of shades of green in nature. Look at all the different shades of green in the leaves used to make this elephant.

Autumn

If it is autumn, you will have a rainbow of leaf colors from which to pick and choose. Although coniferous (evergreen) trees stay green all year round, the leaves of deciduous trees put on quite a flashy show before they fall to the ground.

TRAINING YOUR ARTIST'S EYE

By combining nature's bounty of color in new and creative combinations you can bring your animals vividly to life.

Contrast

Contrast is an important technique to use. Do you see how the owl's bright yellow eyes stand out against the deep green of his body? Yellow and green are contrasting colors because they are so different from each other.

Find strong contrasting colors, and you will see how nature gives us the same reds and browns in leaves as it does in animals' fur and birds' feathers.

Art Notes

Have you thought about where you're going to sit when you work on your leaf animals? It may not seem important, but it is. All artists like to have a space in which they can create. Here are some things that will help you be a better leaf artist.

- A large, flat surface to work on and a comfortable seat.
- A place where you can leave your unfinished art, safe from things like breezes and babies.
- QUIET.

SHAPE AND SIZE

Shape

As you collect your leaves, you'll notice that they come in all different shapes and sizes, as well as different colors: round,

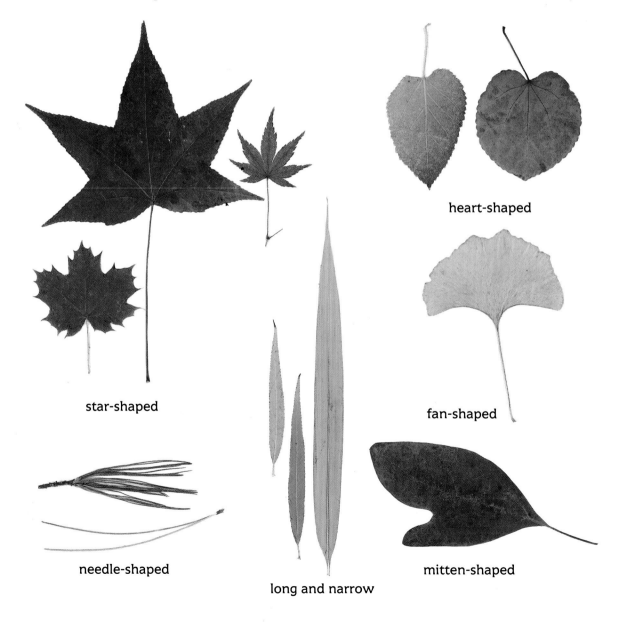

heart-shaped

fan-shaped

star-shaped

mitten-shaped

needle-shaped

long and narrow

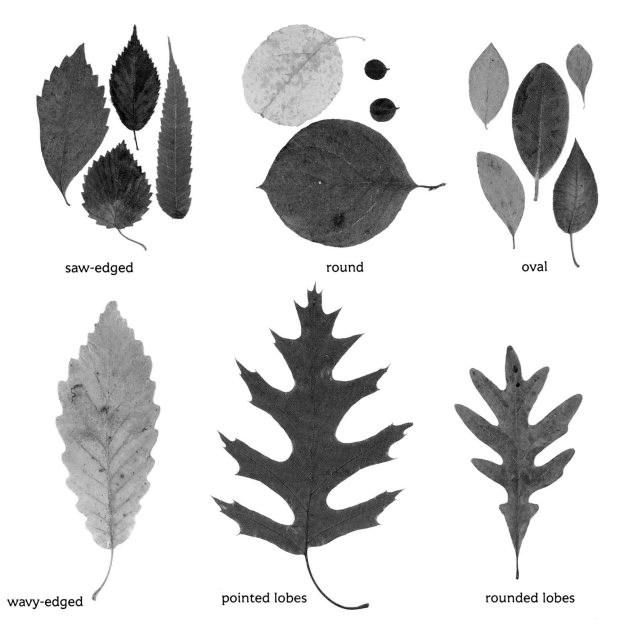

saw-edged

round

oval

wavy-edged

pointed lobes

rounded lobes

oval, long, heart-shaped, and star-shaped. There are even lobed leaves that look like they were cut with scissors.

When you see these different shapes, think about how you can use them when you assemble your leaf animals.

Saw-edged leaves capture the feathers and texture of the rooster's body.

The lobed leaves used for this frog's feet look very realistic.

Long, narrow leaves work well for this fox's legs.

Size

In addition to the colors and shapes of the leaves you collect, you also have to consider their sizes.

The large leaves used to make this cow are perfect for an animal's head and body.

Smaller leaves can then be used for the animal's facial features—like the nose and eyes on this mouse.

Art Notes

Some artists like to have all their materials very carefully arranged before they begin a new work of art. If you think you might be that sort of artist, you could organize your piles by arranging the leaves according to size, or by separating a pile of round leaves into those with smooth edges and those with toothed edges. Stop when you think you'll be able to easily find what you want.

LAYERING

Once you have collected leaves of all colors, shapes, and sizes, you can layer them to create animals that need a more complex design.

The different colors and sizes in this collage blend together to form the flowing, majestic look of this lion's mane.

Famous for its fine plumage, the peacock requires a careful choice of colorful contrasting leaves layered to highlight its brilliant tail.

Art Notes

Many artists need reference materials. That means they need something to look at while they are working. Some artists take photographs of people in different poses and draw from the photos. This helps them capture the image they want.

You might find it useful to have reference materials for your leaf animals. Look in magazines, toy catalogs, greeting cards, and picture books. The picture doesn't have to be of a real animal—it could be a cartoon or a toy. Maybe there is an animal character that you want to try to make, like Babar or Curious George. Never rip anything out of a magazine without getting permission. Your librarian can show you how to copy a picture from a book.

MAKE A SCENE!

Don't limit yourself to designing only one animal at a time.
Once you have some experience making leaf animals, you
may want to try something on a larger scale, like this
underwater scene.

PREPARING THE LEAVES

When you get home, clean the leaves you've collected by soaking them in a bowl of warm water for a few minutes. Blot them dry between two pieces of paper towel. Then place the leaves on two pieces of newspaper. Take care that the leaves do not touch each other, because the parts that overlap will not dry properly. You may also want to trim any stems that are particularly thick. Cover the leaves with another two pieces of newspaper and put something heavy on top. Telephone books or big dictionaries work well. It will take about a week for the leaves to be ready to work with. By then they should be flat, stiff, and dry.

ASSEMBLING THE ANIMALS

Materials

Here are the materials you will need in addition to your leaves.

- Cardboard—The kind from the dry cleaner or laundry with one white side is best. Otherwise, paste colored construction paper onto regular cardboard with a glue stick or a little glue.
- Glue—Rubber cement works best. A glue stick might work, but it can also hurt your leaves. Any water-soluble glue is fine.
- Cotton swabs—Use these to clean up excess glue. They are also good for pushing little leaves into place when your finger feels too big.
- Clear contact paper or heavy-duty plastic wrap.

Putting It All Together

Now that you have all the necessary materials, lay out the leaves on your cardboard, experimenting until you are satisfied with the design. For example, here is how to put a turtle together. Choose a large round leaf for the shell and a small round or oval leaf for the head. Then find four small round leaves for the feet. Last, to give your turtle greater detail, look for four or five small round leaves in a contrasting color to make a pattern on the turtle's shell.

Once you have the design figured out, glue the shell and head leaves to the cardboard. Then paste the other leaves on

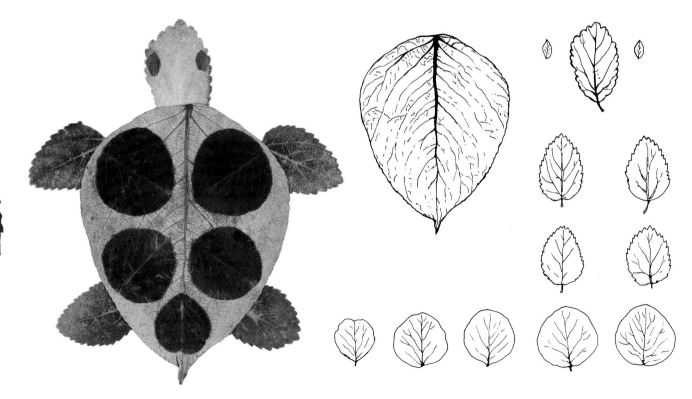

or around these leaves as you have designed them. You can use a damp cotton swab to remove any excess glue. You will soon discover that you don't need to use much glue to get the desired results. Now let your animal dry for one day.

When the animal is dry, cut an oversized plastic sheet or plastic wrap and place it over your board. Fold the edges behind the cardboard and use tape to keep it tight and stretched.

If you want to hang your work, you can glue or tape twine or string to the back of the cardboard, or buy a frame at the store.

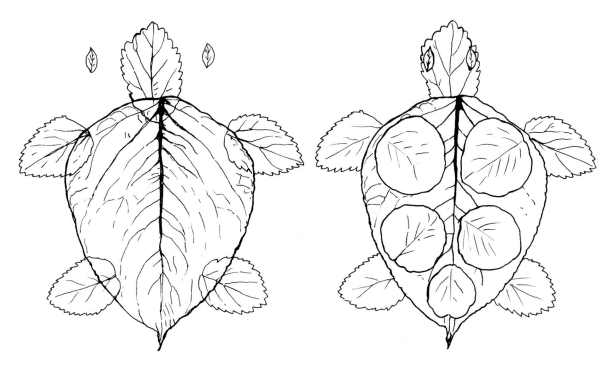

COLLAGE CRAFTS

What can you do with your leaf animals once you've made them? Lots of things. You may find it hard to believe, but adults really do love homemade presents. Here are some ideas.

Stationery   Using large index cards from the stationery store, glue a leaf animal to the side that doesn't have lines. Use your contact paper or plastic wrap to seal it on the card. Make sure to cut the contact paper the same size as the card. On the other side, you could draw a little box where the stamp belongs, in the upper right-hand corner. Make several cards and tie them together with a ribbon.

Ornaments   Cut around your leaf animal, leaving a ¼-inch border around the animal. Tape a piece of string or ribbon to the back of the ornament.

Place mats   Arrange several leaf animals on a large board. You could make your own zoo or farmyard scene. Cover carefully with contact paper or plastic wrap on both sides so it can be wiped clean.

THE LIFE CYCLE OF A LEAF

A leaf starts its life in the spring when it pushes out of buds on a tree branch. Then it begins to make food called sugar sap for the tree. The roots of the tree take water and minerals from the ground and send it up to the leaf. A chemical in the

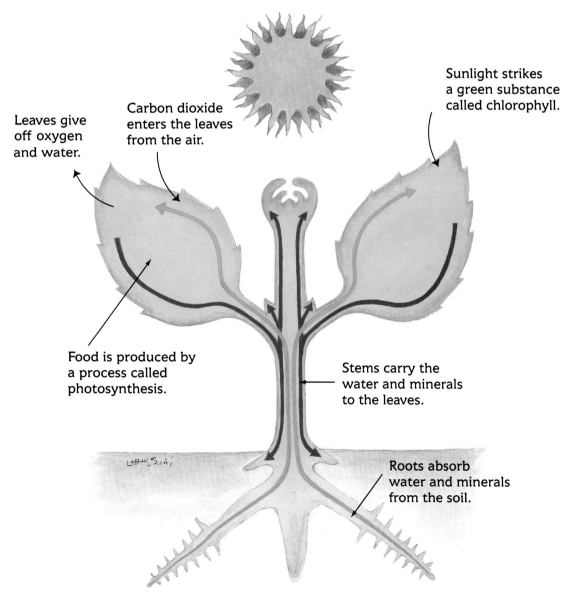

Sunlight strikes a green substance called chlorophyll.

Leaves give off oxygen and water.

Carbon dioxide enters the leaves from the air.

Food is produced by a process called photosynthesis.

Stems carry the water and minerals to the leaves.

Roots absorb water and minerals from the soil.

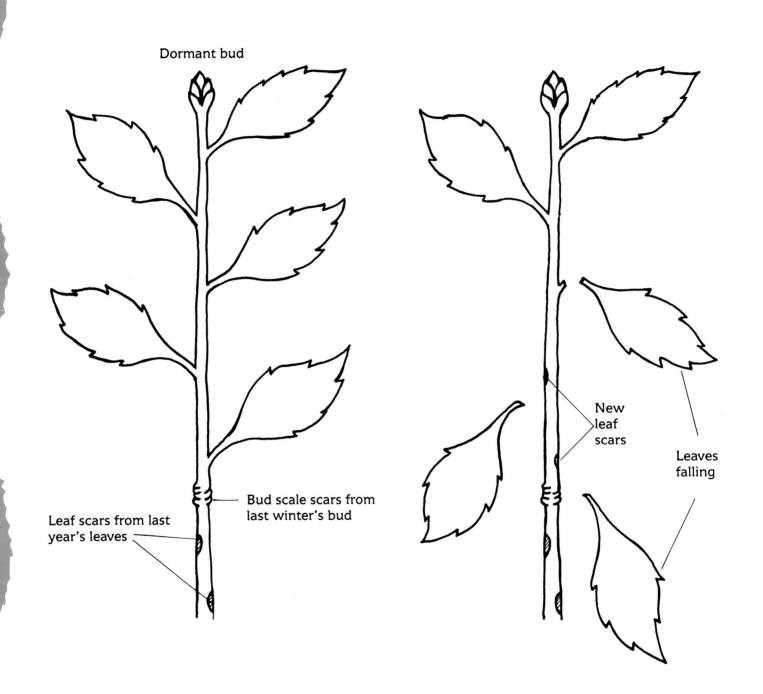

Dormant bud

Bud scale scars from last winter's bud

Leaf scars from last year's leaves

New leaf scars

Leaves falling

leaf called chlorophyll combines the water and minerals with sunshine and carbon dioxide, a gas in the air. This process, called photosynthesis, makes sugar sap. The sap goes through a vein in the leaf stem and into the branches and trunk.

The leaf makes sugar sap all summer long until the air grows cooler and the days get shorter. Then the tree creates a sort of scab where the leaf stem attaches to the branch, so nothing can get in or out of the leaf. Slowly the leaf begins to die. The chlorophyll, which made the leaf green, breaks down and is destroyed, allowing another color to reveal itself. The yellow of poplars, the reds and oranges of maples—all the colors of all the trees have been in the leaves all along, but the green of the chlorophyll kept the colors hidden until now.

Finally the leaf breaks off and falls to the ground, which is why autumn is also called fall. Then rotting leaves and plants replenish the earth with important nutrients. Nature is the world's best recycler.

In the winter, deciduous trees rest. When spring arrives again, the tree begins another season of growth.

FIELD GUIDE

Here are the names, the fall colors, and the approximate sizes of many of the leaves used to make the animals in this book along with the area of the country where they are found.

ARROWWOOD (see Downy Arrowwood)

ASH  (a) *Green ash,* pale to rich yellow; (b) *White ash,* bright colors from yellow to red to brown; 5–13 cm. (2–5 in.) long. Widespread throughout the country, except southern Florida and the West.

BEECH  Rich yellow to bronze; 5–12 cm. (2–4¼ in.) long. Widespread in the East, except southern Florida.

BITTERSWEET  Light yellow; 4–7 cm. (1½–3 in.) diameter. Eastern coastal United States, scattered localities from Connecticut to North Carolina.

BLACK LOCUST  Rich yellow; 20–30 cm. (8–12 in.) long. East central United States, as far north as Michigan.

BLUEBERRY

Glossy maroon or red; 2–8 cm. (1–3 in.) long. Widespread, except in extreme South and West.

BOX ELDER

Yellow, bronze, or brown; 2.5–5 cm. (1–2 in.) long. South Alberta through Ontario and New York, south to southern Texas and central Florida.

DOGWOOD

(a) *Flowering dogwood,* red to maroon; 6–10 cm. (2½–4 in.) long. Found throughout most of the Eastern United States. (b) *Gray dogwood,* red to maroon on upper surface, greenish gray beneath; 4–8 cm. (1½–3 in.) long. Abundant in northern Appalachians, tapering off to the south. (c) *Roughleaf dogwood,* similar to the Gray dogwood, common in the Midwest.

DOWNY ARROWWOOD

Rose to maroon; 4–8 cm. (1½–3 in.) long. Throughout the Appalachians and adjacent foothills.

GINKGO

Yellow; 2.5–5 cm. (1–2 in.) long. Throughout eastern United States and the Pacific coast.

MAPLE

(a) *Red maple,* brilliant red, orange, or yellow; 6–13 cm. (2½–5 in.) long. Easterly: greatest north-south distribution of all East Coast tree species. Through central states, west to eastern Texas. (b) *Sugar maple,* bright yellow, orange, or red; 10–15 cm. (4–6 in.) wide and long. Widespread in north central and northeast zones.

OAK

(a) *Black oak* (or *Yellow oak,* for its yellow-orange inner bark), red, reddish brown, or yellow-brown; 15–20 cm. (6–8 in.) long. Common over much of eastern North America. (b) *Chestnut oak,* brown to bronze-yellow, may also be dull red; 10–20 cm. (4–8 in.) long. Appalachian region, and as far north as southern Ontario. (c) *White oak,* dull red, brown, bronze, or yellow; 10–25 cm. (4–10 in.) long. Extensive range, east and central United States.

POPLAR

Tulip poplar, tall cones of light yellow foliage; 8–20 cm. (3–8 in.) long and wide. Widespread in eastern United States. Not in western and west central zones.

SASSAFRAS

Brilliant yellow, orange, or red; 6–15 cm. (2½–6 in.) long. Throughout most of eastern and central North America.

SHAGBARK HICKORY

Golden yellow; 8–18 cm. (3–7 in.) long. Fairly widespread, except in the West and in extreme north and south zones.

SMOOTH SUMAC

Scarlet leaves; 30 cm. (12 in.) long. Widespread in eastern United States.

SWEETGUM

Dark maroon to brilliant red, soft pink, orange, or clear yellow; 7–15 cm. (3–6 in.) long. Fairly widespread from southern New England south to Florida, west to Texas.

WHITE MULBERRY (or Silk Mulberry)

Bright, glossy yellow; 5–20 cm. (2–8 in.) long. Widespread.